BROWNIES BLONDIES and BARS

BROWNIES BLONDIES and BARS

Stephanie Brubaker

FRONT TABLE BOOKS | AN IMPRINT OF CEDAR FORT, INC. | SPRINGVILLE, UTAH

The opinions and views expressed herein belong solely to the authors and do not necessarily represent the opinions or views of Cedar Fort, Inc. Permission for the use of sources, graphics, and photos is also solely the responsibility of the authors.

ISBN 13: 978-1-4621-1694-2

Published by Front Table Books, an imprint of Cedar Fort, Inc.
2373 W. 700 S., Springville, UT 84663
Distributed by Cedar Fort, Inc., www.cedarfort.com

LIBRARY OF CONGRESS CATALOGING-IN-PUBLICATION DATA

Brubaker, Stephanie, 1983-
Brownies, blondies, and bars / Stephanie Brubaker.
     pages cm
Includes index.
ISBN 978-1-4621-1694-2 (layflat binding : alk. paper)
1. Brownies (Cooking) 2. Bars (Desserts) I. Title.
TX771.B889 2015
641.86'53--dc23

                          2015017578

Cover design by M. Shaun McMurdie
Page design by Rebecca J. Greenwood
Cover design © 2015 by Lyle Mortimer
Edited by Melissa J. Caldwell

Printed in China

10 9 8 7 6 5 4 3 2 1

Printed on acid-free paper

For Jared, my beloved.
I have found the one whom my soul loves . . . I love you most!!
Song of Solomon 2:16

For our children.
You bring immeasurable joy to my heart.
I love you all more than you can ever imagine.

CONTENTS

Acknowledgments xi

Introduction 1

Baking Tips. 3

Brownies

Back for Seconds Brownies .8

Coconut Almond Fudge Brownies 11

Cherry Cordial Brownies. 14

Banana Split Brownies 17

Chocolate Chip Cookie Stuffed Brownies 20

Coconut Macaroon Brownies 23

Coffee Toffee Brownies with Nutella Frosting 26

Dark Chocolate Raspberry Brownies. 29

Glazed Lemon Brownies 32

Mint Fudge Stuffed Brownies 35

Nutella Brownies with a Pretzel Crust 38

Oreo Mousse Brownies 41

Hot Fudge Peanut Butter Cup Cheesecake Brownies 44

S'mores Brownies 47

Toffee Cheesecake Brownies 50

Peanut Butter Supreme Brownies 53

Triple Chocolate Brownies with Whipped Ganache 56

White Chocolate Fudge Brownies 59

Blondies

Apple Peanut Butter Blondies with Caramel Peanut Butter Sauce 64

Caramel Peanut Blondies with Chocolate Ganache 67

Marshmallow Butterscotch Blondies 68

Chocolate-Covered Potato Chip Blondies 70

Cinnamon Roll Blondies 73

Cranberry Orange Blondies 76

Fluffernutter Chocolate Chip Blondies 79

M&M Pretzel Blondies 81

Peanut Butter Cinnamon Blondies 83

Pumpkin Peanut Butter Cheesecake Blondies 84

Maple Pecan Blondies 87

Snickerdoodle Blondies 91

Magic Blondie Bars 93

Bars

Brown Butter Oatmeal Raisin Bars 97

Brownie Stuffed Krispie Treats with Salted Caramel 99

Cannoli Cream Cookie Bars 103

Chocolate Carmelitas 105

Chocolate Cheesecake Cookie Bars 108

Cinnamon Swirl Bars 111

No Bake Oreo Peanut Butter Cheesecake Bars 114

Chocolate Pecan Pie Bars 116

Lemon Blueberry Cream Bars 119

Neapolitan Cookie Bars 121

Eggnog Meltaway Bars 125

Funfetti Cream Cheese Bars 126

No Bake Peanut Butter Cup Bars with Oreo Crust 129

Peanut Butter Fudge Bars 130

Peppermint Mocha Bars 133

Red Velvet Chocolate Chip Bars 136

S'mores Bars 138

Toasted Coconut Lime Cheesecake Bars 140

White Chocolate Dipped Molasses Bars 143

Index 146

About the Author 148

ACKNOWLEDGMENTS

I would like to thank my husband, Jared, who always believes in me and encourages me to follow my dreams, even when it seems impossible. I could not have written this book without his support. I love you!

To my daughter, Isabella (6), who was cheering me on throughout this whole process. She is always eager to help in the kitchen—and even more eager to taste test. She always has something positive to say and makes me feel like I can do anything.

To my son Xander (3), who is my #1 helper in the kitchen. He loves baking and has helped me make many of the recipes in this book with much joy and excitement!

To my son Kingston (3), who is always the first in line to taste test a new recipe. Throughout the process of writing this book and developing these recipes, he could be found at my feet asking, "Can I taste yet?"

To my son Asher (1), who would happily sit in his highchair and watch me bake, or play at my feet pulling every pot and pan out of my cabinets as I worked. Even when he just wanted to snuggle, I gained extra muscle and learned how to bake so many things with just one hand.

To my unborn baby, who held off on giving me morning sickness until after I finished testing and retesting every recipe (thank you!!!). You have many brownies, blondies, and bars to look forward to when you're older!

To my family, neighbors, friends, and church family, who gladly taste tested my recipes and gave me honest feedback. I could never have eaten all these bars myself, so thank you! And a big thanks to everyone who encouraged me and cheered me on, especially on the hard days. Thank you for believing in me.

And, finally, thank you to my Cedar Fort family for helping make my dream of writing this book a reality.

INTRODUCTION

Ever since I was little, I have loved to bake. I remember helping my mother make cookies and praying she wouldn't notice how many chocolate chips I "spilled" on the counter when trying to pour them into the mixing bowl (because everyone knows, if you spill them, you get to eat them). When I was a little older, around nine or ten, I started baking all on my own. I found it so exciting to make cakes or cookies or brownies out of practically nothing!

Brownies have always been my favorite. I would request them for my birthday instead of cake! I remember one day in particular, when I was about eleven years old, our pastor and his family were coming over to our house for dinner, and I was in charge of making the dessert. Yippee! I chose to make brownies, of course. This time though, I wasn't paying close attention to the recipe, and I realized after I put them in the oven that I did not make them according to the instructions. I was so nervous because company was coming and my brownies were going to be awful.

Except they weren't!

They were chewier and fudgier and more delicious than any other time I had made them, and they were a huge hit with everyone that night.

From that day on I became known for my brownies. That recipe slipup gave me the freedom and confidence to be creative and to not follow every recipe. In fact, I almost never used a recipe again. I played around with methods that I knew would work and started tinkering with them to make them my own. Every family gathering became a new chance for me to experiment and create something that was all mine.

As much fun as it was to bake without recipes, and add a little of this and a little of that instead of actually measuring, there was a problem. I was often asked for the recipe for whatever dessert I had come up with, and I couldn't give one! I wasn't being rude or secretive—I honestly didn't have a recipe. I could tell them what I put in it, but not how much. I couldn't even say how long it cooked because I would just keep checking the oven every few minutes to see if my creation was ready.

This is how my website *Back for Seconds* (and eventually, this cookbook) was born.

I was determined to measure and keep careful track of everything that went into the mixing bowls. I took pictures of the finished products and started sharing them with my recipes a few times a week. From then on, I would have an answer when someone asked for one of my recipes. Yes, I do have the recipe and you can find it on my website.

Back for Seconds has grown in popularity over the past three years, and I am having as much fun as ever experimenting in the kitchen. Now I have four cute little kitchen helpers of my own (with another one on the way), and it brings me much happiness to see their excitement being in the kitchen too. It's really quite thrilling to take ordinary ingredients and put them together to make something extraordinary.

While I have expanded my repertoire to include much more than just sweet treats (my family seems to enjoy eating actual meals every day) brownies will always be my favorite.

I hope these recipes put a smile on your face. I hope you bake some of these brownies with friends, family, or your children, and I hope you have FUN and make some memories together! I know the times that I am in the kitchen with my little ones, we are creating more than just yummy food; we are making memories that we will all keep with us forever. I cherish those times!

I hope you will make these brownies, blondies, and bars, and share them with the ones you love. Share them with a neighbor, or bring them to a potluck or a party. Bring a smile to someone's face.

These recipes were a labor of love and were so much fun for me to develop, and I hope you can taste it in each bite!

I don't know which recipe you'll try first, but I do know you'll be back for seconds!

XOXO,

Stephanie

backforseconds.com

BAKING *Tips*

The wonderful thing about the recipes in this book is they are all easy to make. Some of them require a few more steps than others but none of them are difficult. I wanted to include a few little tips that will help ensure the process of making these recipes goes as smoothly as possible and has a wonderful outcome!

TIP #1

Use a spoon to scoop flour into your measuring cup, and then level it off with the back of a knife. Never pack flour into a measuring cup. It should be nice and light!

TIP #2

Brown sugar should always be packed tightly into a measuring cup, unless otherwise stated in a recipe.

TIP #3

Use an offset spatula to evenly spread batter into the pan.

TIP #4

Always read through the recipe completely before starting. You want to be sure you have all of the ingredients on hand and that you understand all of the steps and baking and chill times before you get started.

TIP #5

Line your pan with foil! Sure, you could just grease your pan and skip the foil, but you will regret it when you are trying to dig out the first brownie and it starts to break apart.

Just take a long piece of foil and line the pan, leaving enough excess to hang over the sides by a couple of inches. Then spray the foil with non-stick baking spray. Now when it is time to cut the brownies, you can just lift them out of the pan using the foil as handles. Peel back the foil, and you can make nice, cleanly cut squares.

TIP #6

Chill the bars thoroughly before cutting. Once the bars have cooled, place them in the refrigerator for a few hours. Once they are completely chilled, lift them from the pan using the foil handles. Peel back the foil and use a long sharp knife to cut your bars into even squares.

TIP #7

Use a plastic knife to cut the bars. If you don't have time, or don't want to chill the bars before cutting, use a plastic knife instead of a metal one. The brownies and bars are less likely to stick to the plastic knife, giving you a cleaner cut.

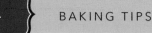

Every oven is different. Check your bars a few minutes before the suggested baking time. You can always bake them longer, but once you've overbaked them, nothing can be done. I tend to like my bars a little on the less-done side, so I always test them a couple minutes before the recipe says. Some people may prefer a more well-done bar, so you may need to bake them a couple minutes longer than the suggested time. Every oven is different and every person has different preferences. The key is to keep a close eye on the bars to get the outcome you desire.

Last, I have an unofficial, off-the-record tip, just between us—you can never have too much chocolate!

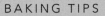

CHAPTER ONE

Brownies

BACK FOR SECONDS *Brownies*

These brownies, I truly believe, are the best brownies ever!
They are rich, moist, chewy on the edges, and so fudgy.

Ingredients

1 cup (2 sticks) unsalted butter

1¼ cup semisweet chocolate chips

¾ cup unsweetened cocoa powder

2 cups sugar

¼ cup brown sugar

1 tsp. vanilla extract

½ tsp. salt

4 eggs

1¼ cups flour

Directions

1. Preheat oven to 350°F.

2. Line a 9 × 13 baking pan with foil, leaving enough to hang over the edges. Spray lightly with cooking spray.

3. Fill a saucepan about 2 inches with water. Place a heat-safe bowl over the pan, making sure the bottom of the bowl does not touch the water. Heat the water on low until just simmering. Place butter and chocolate in the bowl, stirring constantly until mostly melted. Remove from heat and stir until completely melted and smooth.*

4. Stir in cocoa powder until completely incorporated. Add sugar, brown sugar, vanilla, and salt, stirring to combine. Stir in eggs, one at a time until completely mixed through. Gently stir in flour until just incorporated and no more flour is visible. The batter will be thick.

5. Spread batter evenly into the pan and bake on the center rack for 24–28 minutes or until a tester toothpick inserted into the center of the brownies comes out clean or with fudgy crumbs.

6. Allow to cool completely. Store in sealed container. Makes 28 brownies.

*You can also use the microwave to melt the chocolate. Place butter and chocolate chips in a glass mixing bowl and heat in the microwave in 30-second intervals, stirring between each burst, until melted and smooth.

COCONUT ALMOND *Fudge Brownies*

These brownies are like an Almond Joy candy bar in brownie form.
Chewy, fudgy, and completely delicious!

Ingredients

1 cup (2 sticks) unsalted butter

1¼ cups semisweet chocolate chips

¾ cup unsweetened cocoa powder

2 cups sugar

¼ cup brown sugar

1 tsp. vanilla extract

½ tsp. salt

4 eggs

1¼ cups flour

1 cup sliced almonds

1½ cups sweetened flaked coconut

Directions

1. Preheat oven to 350°F.

2. Line a 9 × 13 baking pan with foil, leaving enough to hang over the edges. Spray lightly with cooking spray.

3. Fill a saucepan with about 2 inches of water. Place a heat-safe bowl over the pan, making sure the bottom of the bowl does not touch the water. Heat the water on low until just simmering. Place butter and chocolate in the bowl, stirring constantly until mostly melted. Remove from heat, and stir until completely melted and smooth.*

4. Stir in cocoa powder until completely incorporated. Add sugar, brown sugar, vanilla, and salt, stirring to combine. Stir in eggs, one at a time until completely mixed through. Gently stir in flour until just incorporated and no more flour is visible. Stir in almonds and coconut. The batter will be thick.

5. Spread batter evenly into the pan and bake on the center rack for 24–28 minutes or until a tester inserted into the center of the brownies comes out clean or with fudgy crumbs.

6. Allow to cool completely. Store in sealed container. Makes 28 brownies.

*You can also use the microwave to melt the chocolate. Place butter and chocolate chips in a glass mixing bowl and heat in the microwave in 30-second intervals, stirring between each burst, until melted and smooth.

CHERRY CORDIAL *Brownies*

If you like cherry cordials, you will love these brownies! Maraschino cherries are studded throughout these fudgy brownies with a sweet cherry frosting and, of course, a cherry on top!

Ingredients

BROWNIES

1 cup (2 sticks) unsalted butter

1¼ cups semisweet chocolate chips

¾ cup unsweetened cocoa powder

2 cups sugar

¼ cup brown sugar

2 Tbsp. juice from maraschino cherry jar

½ tsp. salt

4 eggs

1 (10-oz.) jar maraschino cherries, drained (saving the juice) and chopped

1½ cups flour

FROSTING

½ cup (1 stick) unsalted butter, softened

2½ cup powdered sugar

dash of salt

2-4 Tbsp. juice from maraschino cherry jar

Note

I like to serve these topped with long stemmed maraschino cherries. It's not necessary, but it makes for a nice presentation.

Directions

1. Preheat oven to 350°F

2. Line a 9 × 13 baking pan with foil, leaving enough to hang over the edges. Spray lightly with cooking spray.

BROWNIES

3. Fill a saucepan about 2 inches with water. Place a heat-safe bowl over the pan, making sure the bottom of the bowl does not touch the water. Heat the water on low until just simmering. Place butter and chocolate in the bowl, stirring constantly until mostly melted. Remove from heat and stir until completely melted and smooth.*

4. Stir in cocoa powder until completely incorporated. Add sugar, brown sugar, cherry juice, and salt, stirring to combine. Stir in eggs, one at a time until completely mixed through. Stir in cherries. Gently stir in flour until just incorporated and no more flour is visible. The batter will be thick.

5. Spread batter evenly into the pan and bake on the center rack for 28–30 minutes or until a tester inserted into the center of the brownies comes out clean or with fudgy crumbs.

6. Allow to cool completely before frosting.

FROSTING

7. In a mixing bowl, beat the butter until creamy. Add the sugar, salt, and 2 tablespoons cherry juice, and beat until light and fluffy. If too thick, add more cherry juice, 1 tablespoon at a time until desired consistency is reached.

8. Store refrigerated in sealed container. Makes 28 brownies.

*You can also use the microwave to melt the chocolate. Place butter and chocolate chips in a glass mixing bowl and heat in the microwave in 30-second intervals, stirring between each burst, until melted and smooth.

BANANA SPLIT *Brownies*

The classic ice-cream treat meets banana brownies, and the result is amazing!

Ingredients

BANANA BROWNIES

¾ cup (1½ sticks) unsalted butter, softened (divided)

8 oz. white chocolate chips

1½ cups bananas, mashed (3 large bananas)

1⅓ cups sugar

3 eggs

1 tsp. vanilla extract

½ tsp. salt

2¼ cups flour

FROSTING

½ cup (1 stick) unsalted butter, softened

¾ cup unsweetened cocoa powder

2 cups powdered sugar

4–6 Tbsp. cream

TOPPINGS

2¼ cups sliced strawberries, patted dry

¾ cup chopped walnuts

Note

If making in advance or if the whole recipe won't be consumed the day of baking, leave off strawberries until ready to serve. Just sprinkle on top!

BANANA SPLIT *Brownies* CONTINUED

Directions

1. Preheat oven to 350°F.

2. Line a 9 × 13 baking pan with foil, leaving enough to hang over the edges. Spray lightly with cooking spray.

BANANA BROWNIES

3. Fill a saucepan with about 2 inches of water. Place a heat-safe bowl over the pan, making sure the bottom of the bowl does not touch the water. Heat the water on low until just simmering. Place 1 stick of butter and white chocolate in the bowl, stirring constantly until mostly melted. Remove from heat and stir until completely melted and smooth.*

4. Stir in remaining softened butter until mixed through. Add bananas and sugar, and mix until combined. Mix in eggs, one at a time, and then stir in vanilla and salt. Gently stir in flour until just incorporated and no more flour is visible.

5. Spread batter evenly into the pan and bake on the center rack for 25 minutes or until a tester inserted into the center of the brownies comes out clean. Allow to cool completely.

TOPPINGS

6. Place sliced strawberries in an even layer over cooled brownies. Set aside.

FROSTING

7. In a mixing bowl beat butter, cocoa powder, sugar, and 4 tablespoons cream until smooth and creamy. If too thick, add more cream 1 tablespoon at a time until desired consistency is reached. Carefully spread over strawberries. Immediately sprinkle with walnuts.

8. Store in sealed container. Makes 28 brownies

*You can also use the microwave to melt the chocolate. Place butter and white chocolate chips in a glass mixing bowl and heat in the microwave in 30-second intervals, stirring between each burst, until melted and smooth.

CHOCOLATE CHIP COOKIE *Stuffed Brownies*

Two of my favorite desserts join forces in one of the most irresistible brownies ever!

Ingredients

COOKIE DOUGH

6 Tbsp. unsalted butter, softened

½ cup sugar

¼ cup brown sugar

1 egg

½ tsp. vanilla

¼ tsp. salt

½ tsp. baking soda

1 cup flour

¾ cup mini chocolate chips

BROWNIES

1 cup (2 sticks) unsalted butter

1¼ cups semisweet chocolate chips

¾ cup unsweetened cocoa powder

2 cups sugar

¼ cup brown sugar

1 tsp. vanilla extract

½ tsp. salt

4 eggs

1¼ cups flour

> You may have some remaining cookie dough—just bake them on a cookie sheet at 350°F for 7–8 minutes and enjoy! (This is the bake time for 1-inch dough balls.)

Directions

COOKIE DOUGH

1. In a mixing bowl, cream together the butter and sugars. Add the egg, vanilla, and salt, and mix well. Add the baking soda and flour, and mix until combined. Stir in chocolate chips. Roll into 24 1-inch balls and place on a cookie sheet. Freeze for at least 1 hour.

BROWNIES

2. Preheat oven to 350°F.

3. Line a 9 × 13 baking pan with foil, leaving enough to hang over the edges. Spray lightly with cooking spray.

4. Fill a saucepan with about 2 inches of water. Place a heat-safe bowl over the pan, making sure the bottom of the bowl does not touch the water. Heat the water on low until just simmering. Place butter and chocolate in the bowl, stirring constantly until mostly melted. Remove from heat and stir until completely melted and smooth.*

5. Stir in cocoa powder until completely incorporated. Add sugar, brown sugar, vanilla, and salt, stirring to combine. Stir in eggs, one at a time until completely mixed through. Gently stir in flour until just incorporated and no more flour is visible. The batter will be thick.

6. Spread batter evenly into the pan and bake on the center rack for 15 minutes. Pull from the oven and evenly place the 24 cookie dough balls into the brownies. Continue baking for 20 minutes or until a tester inserted into the center of the brownies comes out clean or with fudgy crumbs.

7. Allow to cool completely. Store in sealed container. Makes 24 brownies.

*You can also use the microwave to melt the chocolate. Place butter and chocolate chips in a glass mixing bowl and heat in the microwave in 30-second intervals, stirring between each burst, until melted and smooth.

COCONUT MACAROON *Brownies*

A thick layer of chewy coconut macaroons adorns rich, decadent brownies in this double-decker delight!

Ingredients

BROWNIES

1 cup (2 sticks) unsalted butter

1¼ cups semisweet chocolate chips

¾ cup unsweetened cocoa powder

2 cups sugar

¼ cup brown sugar

1 tsp. vanilla extract

½ tsp. salt

4 eggs

1¼ cups flour

MACAROONS

3 eggs

1 cup sugar

1 tsp. vanilla extract

1½ cups flour

3½ cups sweetened shredded coconut, divided

Directions

1. Preheat oven to 350°F

2. Line a 9 × 13 baking pan with foil leaving enough to hang over the edges. Spray lightly with cooking spray.

BROWNIES

3. Fill a saucepan with about 2 inches of water. Place a heat-safe bowl over the pan, making sure the bottom of the bowl does not touch the water. Heat the water on low until just simmering. Place butter and chocolate in the bowl, stirring constantly until mostly melted. Remove from heat and stir until completely melted and smooth.*

4. Stir in cocoa powder until completely incorporated. Add sugar, brown sugar, vanilla, and salt, stirring to combine. Stir in eggs, one at a time until completely mixed through. Gently stir in flour until just incorporated and no more flour is visible. The batter will be thick.

5. Spread batter evenly into the pan and bake on the center rack for 10 minutes.

MACAROONS

6. In a mixing bowl combine eggs, sugar, vanilla, flour, and 3 cups of coconut. Drop by spoonfuls over brownie layer, and very carefully spread into an even layer. Sprinkle remaining coconut on top and bake 30–35 more minutes.

7. Allow to cool completely. Store in sealed container. Makes 32 brownies.

*You can also use the microwave to melt the chocolate. Place butter and chocolate chips in a glass mixing bowl and heat in the microwave in 30-second intervals, stirring between each burst, until melted and smooth.

COFFEE TOFFEE BROWNIES *with Nutella Frosting*

I could eat these brownies every day. The coffee really enhances the chocolate flavor, and the creamy frosting sprinkled with crunchy toffee on top is simply irresistible!

Ingredients

BROWNIES

1 cup (2 sticks) unsalted butter

1¼ cups semisweet chocolate chips

¾ cup unsweetened cocoa powder

2 cups sugar

¼ cup brown sugar

1 Tbsp. strong brewed coffee

1 tsp. vanilla extract

½ tsp. salt

4 eggs

1¼ cups flour

1 cup Heath toffee baking bits

FROSTING

¼ cup (4 Tbsp.) unsalted butter, softened

½ cup Nutella

½ cup cocoa powder

2 cups powdered sugar

3-4 Tbsp. strong brewed coffee, cooled

TOPPING

1 cup Heath toffee baking bits

Directions

1. Preheat oven to 350°F.

2. Line a 9 × 13 baking pan with foil, leaving enough to hang over the edges. Spray lightly with cooking spray.

BROWNIES

3. Fill a saucepan with about 2 inches of water. Place a heat-safe bowl over the pan, making sure the bottom of the bowl does not touch the water. Heat the water on low until just simmering. Place butter and chocolate in the bowl, stirring constantly until mostly melted. Remove from heat, and stir until completely melted and smooth.*

4. Stir in cocoa powder until completely incorporated. Add sugar, brown sugar, coffee, vanilla, and salt, stirring to combine. Stir in eggs, one at a time until completely mixed through. Gently stir in flour until just incorporated and no more flour is visible. The batter will be thick. Stir in Heath bits.

5. Spread batter evenly into the prepared pan and bake on the center rack for 25–30 minutes or until a tester inserted into the center of the brownies comes out clean or with fudgy crumbs.

6. Allow to cool completely.

FROSTING

7. In a mixing bowl, beat the butter and Nutella until smooth. Add cocoa and powdered sugar with 2 tablespoons of coffee and mix well. Add more coffee 1 tablespoon at a time until desired consistency is reached.

8. Spread over cooled brownies and sprinkle with Heath bits.

*You can also use the microwave to melt the chocolate. Place butter and chocolate chips in a glass mixing bowl and heat in the microwave in 30-second intervals, stirring between each burst, until melted and smooth.

DARK CHOCOLATE *Raspberry Brownies*

Deep, dark, rich brownies with bright raspberries swirled throughout, baked on top of a buttery shortbread crust!

Ingredients

CRUST

¾ cup (1½ sticks) unsalted butter, cold and cubed

1 cup powdered sugar

2 cups flour

BROWNIES

1 cup (2 sticks) unsalted butter

1¼ cups semisweet chocolate chips

¾ cup dark cocoa powder

2 cups sugar

¼ cup brown sugar

1 tsp. vanilla extract

½ tsp. salt

4 eggs

1¼ cups flour

1½ cups fresh raspberries, divided

½ cup mini chocolate chips

Directions

1. Preheat oven to 350°F.

2. Line a 9 × 13 baking pan with foil, leaving enough to hang over the edges. Spray lightly with cooking spray.

CRUST

3. In a food processor, pulse together the butter, sugar, and flour until the butter is evenly distributed. Press evenly into the prepared pan and bake 8 minutes.

BROWNIES

4. Fill a saucepan with about 2 inches of water. Place a heat-safe bowl over the pan, making sure the bottom of the bowl does not touch the water. Heat the water on low until just simmering. Place butter and chocolate in the bowl, stirring constantly until mostly melted. Remove from heat, and stir until completely melted and smooth.*

5. Stir in cocoa powder until completely incorporated. Add sugar, brown sugar, vanilla, and salt, stirring to combine. Stir in eggs, one at a time until completely mixed through. Gently stir in flour until just incorporated and no more flour is visible. Stir in 1 cup of the raspberries.

6. Spread batter evenly over the crust and sprinkle mini chocolate chips and remaining raspberries over the top. Bake on the center rack for 30–35 minutes or until a tester inserted into the center of the brownies comes out clean or with fudgy crumbs.

7. Allow to cool completely before cutting into bars. Store in sealed container. Makes 28 brownies.

*You can also use the microwave to melt the chocolate. Place butter and chocolate chips in a glass mixing bowl and heat in the microwave in 30-second intervals, stirring between each burst, until melted and smooth.

GLAZED LEMON *Brownies*

These are a lemon lover's dream!
So chewy and fudgy and bursting with bright lemon flavor in every bite.

Ingredients

BROWNIES

¾ cup (1½ sticks) unsalted butter

8 oz. white chocolate chips

1⅓ cups sugar

¼ cup lemon juice

3 eggs

½ tsp. salt

zest of 3 lemons, divided

2¼ cups flour

GLAZE

2 cups powdered sugar

1-2 Tbsp. milk

Directions

1. Preheat oven to 350°F.

2. Line a 9 × 13 baking pan with foil, leaving enough to hang over the edges. Spray lightly with cooking spray.

BROWNIES

3. Fill a saucepan with about 2 inches of water. Place a heat-safe bowl over the pan, making sure the bottom of the bowl does not touch the water. Heat the water on low until just simmering. Place butter and white chocolate chips in the bowl, stirring constantly until mostly melted. Remove from heat and stir until completely melted and smooth.*

4. Stir in sugar and lemon juice. Mix in eggs, one at a time until completely mixed through. Stir in the salt and half of the lemon zest. Gently stir in flour until just incorporated and no more flour is visible.

5. Spread batter evenly into the pan and bake on the center rack for 20 minutes or until a tester inserted into the center of the brownies comes out clean or with fudgy crumbs. Do not overbake or they will dry out and no longer be fudgy like a brownie.

6. Allow to cool completely.

GLAZE

7. In a bowl whisk together powdered sugar and 1 tablespoon milk until smooth and thin enough to spread. Add more milk 1 teaspoon at a time if needed. Pour over brownies and sprinkle with remaining zest.

8. Store in sealed container (I like them refrigerated). Makes 28 brownies.

*You can also use the microwave to melt the white chocolate. Place butter and white chocolate chips in a glass mixing bowl and heat in the microwave in 30-second intervals, stirring between each burst, until melted and smooth.

MINT FUDGE STUFFED *Brownies*

These indulgent brownies are the supreme mint-chocolate dessert.
Perfect at Christmas time or any time the craving hits!

Ingredients

BROWNIES

1 cup (2 sticks) unsalted butter

1¼ cups semisweet chocolate chips

¾ cup unsweetened cocoa powder

2 cups sugar

¼ cup brown sugar

1 tsp. vanilla extract

½ tsp. salt

4 eggs

1¼ cups flour

MINT FUDGE

2½ cups white chocolate chips

1 cup sweetened condensed milk

1½ tsp. mint extract

6 drops green food coloring (optional)

TOPPING

1 cup Andes Mints (I use the bag of chopped mints)

Note

Be careful when spreading each layer into the pan not to disturb the layer below. I find it easiest to pour or spoon the batter as evenly as possible to avoid having to do too much spreading.

Directions

1. Preheat oven to 350°F.

2. Line a 9 × 13 baking pan with foil, leaving enough to hang over the edges. Spray lightly with cooking spray.

BROWNIES

3. Fill a saucepan with about 2 inches of water. Place a heat-safe bowl over the pan, making sure the bottom of the bowl does not touch the water. Heat the water on low until just simmering. Place butter and chocolate in the bowl, stirring constantly until mostly melted. Remove from heat, and stir until completely melted and smooth.*

4. Stir in cocoa powder until completely incorporated. Add sugar, brown sugar, vanilla, and salt, stirring to combine. Stir in eggs, one at a time until completely mixed through. Gently stir in flour until just incorporated and no more flour is visible. The batter will be thick.

MINT FUDGE

5. In a separate bowl, heat the white chocolate and condensed milk in the microwave in 30-second intervals, stirring between each burst, until melted and smooth. Add mint and food coloring, and stir to combine.

6. Spread half of the brownie batter evenly into the prepared pan, and carefully spread the fudge on top. Gently spread the remaining brownie batter over the fudge.

TOPPING

7. Sprinkle evenly with mints and bake on the center rack for 30–35 minutes or until brownies are set and edges start to slightly pull away from the pan.

8. Allow to cool, and then refrigerate until completely set, at least 2 hours. Makes 32 brownies.

*You can also use the microwave to melt the chocolate. Place butter and chocolate chips in a glass mixing bowl and heat in the microwave in 30-second intervals, stirring between each burst, until melted and smooth.

NUTELLA *Brownies with a Pretzel Crust*

Sweet and salty, crunchy and chewy—these brownies have it all!

Ingredients

CRUST

2 cups crushed pretzels

5 Tbsp. unsalted butter, melted

BROWNIES

1 cup (2 sticks) unsalted butter

1¼ cups semisweet chocolate chips

⅓ cup Nutella

¾ cup unsweetened cocoa powder

2 cups sugar

¼ cup brown sugar

1 tsp. vanilla extract

½ tsp. salt

4 eggs

1½ cups flour

FROSTING

½ cup unsalted butter, softened

⅓ cup Nutella

½ cup unsweetened cocoa powder

2 cups powdered sugar

4-6 Tbsp cream

TOPPING

¼ cup caramel sauce

¼ tsp. sea salt

Note

Be careful when spreading brownie batter over the crust. I find it easiest to pour or spoon the batter as evenly as possible to avoid having to do too much spreading.

Directions

1. Preheat oven to 350°F.

2. Line a 9 × 13 baking pan with foil, leaving enough to hang over the edges. Spray lightly with cooking spray.

CRUST

3. In a bowl, stir together the pretzels with the melted butter. Press into the prepared pan. Set aside.

BROWNIES

4. Fill a saucepan with about 2 inches of water. Place a heat-safe bowl over the pan, making sure the bottom of the bowl does not touch the water. Heat the water on low until just simmering. Place butter and chocolate in the bowl, stirring constantly until mostly melted. Remove from heat, and stir until completely melted and smooth.*

5. Stir in Nutella and cocoa powder until completely incorporated. Add sugar, brown sugar, vanilla, and salt, stirring to combine. Stir in eggs, one at a time until completely mixed through. Gently stir in flour until just incorporated and no more flour is visible. The batter will be thick.

6. Very carefully spread batter evenly over the crust, and bake on the center rack for 28–30 minutes or until a tester inserted into the center of the brownies comes out clean or with fudgy crumbs.

7. Allow to cool completely before frosting.

FROSTING

8. In a mixing bowl, beat together the butter and Nutella until light and smooth. Add cocoa, sugar, and 4 tablespoons cream, and beat until fluffy and smooth. If too thick, add more cream 1 tablespoon at a time until desired consistency is reached.

TOPPING

9. For the topping, heat the caramel until thin enough to drizzle. Stir in the sea salt and drizzle over brownies.

10. Store in sealed container. Makes 32 brownies.

*You can also use the microwave to melt the chocolate. Place butter and chocolate chips in a glass mixing bowl and heat in the microwave in 30-second intervals, stirring between each burst, until melted and smooth.

OREO MOUSSE *Brownies*

These brownies are always a huge hit. Creamy mousse loaded with Oreos on top of perfectly fudgy cookies-and-cream brownies. What could be better?

Ingredients

BROWNIES

1 cup (2 sticks) unsalted butter

1¼ cups semisweet chocolate chips

¾ cup unsweetened cocoa powder

2 cups sugar

¼ cup brown sugar

1 tsp. vanilla extract

½ tsp. salt

4 eggs

1¼ cups flour

1½ cups chopped Oreos (14 cookies)

MOUSSE

8 oz. cream cheese, softened

1½ cups powdered sugar

8 oz. Cool Whip, thawed

2 cups Oreos finely chopped (20 Oreos)

Directions

1. Preheat oven to 350°F.

2. Line a 9 × 13 baking pan with foil, leaving enough to hang over the edges. Spray lightly with cooking spray.

BROWNIES

3. Fill a saucepan with about 2 inches of water. Place a heat-safe bowl over the pan, making sure the bottom of the bowl does not touch the water. Heat the water on low until just simmering. Place butter and chocolate in the bowl, stirring constantly until mostly melted. Remove from heat, and stir until completely melted and smooth.*

4. Stir in cocoa powder until completely incorporated. Add sugar, brown sugar, vanilla, and salt, stirring to combine. Stir in eggs, one at a time until completely mixed through. Gently stir in flour until just incorporated and no more flour is visible. Stir in chopped Oreos.

5. Spread batter evenly into the pan and bake on the center rack for 24–28 minutes or until a tester inserted into the center of the brownies comes out clean or with fudgy crumbs.

6. Allow to cool completely before topping with mousse.

MOUSSE

7. In a mixing bowl, beat together the cream cheese and powdered sugar until light and smooth. Gently stir in the Cool Whip, and then fold in the Oreos. Spread over cooled brownies.

8. Store refrigerated in sealed container. Makes 32 brownies.

*You can also use the microwave to melt the chocolate. Place butter and chocolate chips in a glass mixing bowl and heat in the microwave in 30-second intervals, stirring between each burst, until melted and smooth

HOT FUDGE PEANUT BUTTER CUP
Cheesecake Brownies

These ultra rich brownies are unbelievably scrumptious! The name says it all!

Ingredients

BROWNIES

1 cup (2 sticks) unsalted butter

1¼ cups semisweet chocolate chips

¾ cup unsweetened cocoa powder

2 cups sugar

¼ cup brown sugar

1 tsp. vanilla extract

½ tsp. salt

4 eggs

1¼ cups flour

HOT FUDGE LAYER

8 oz. cream cheese

1 jar (16-oz.) hot fudge

TOPPING

1½ cups chopped peanut butter cups (about 30 mini cups)

Note

Be careful when spreading each layer into the pan to not disturb the layer below. I find it easiest to pour or spoon the batter as evenly as possible to avoid having to do too much spreading.

HOT FUDGE PEANUT BUTTER CUP
Cheesecake Brownies CONTINUED
Directions

1. Preheat oven to 350°F.
2. Line a 9 × 13 baking pan with foil, leaving enough to hang over the edges. Spray lightly with cooking spray.

BROWNIES

3. Place butter and chocolate chips in a glass mixing bowl and heat in the microwave in 30-second intervals, stirring between each burst, until melted and smooth.
4. Stir in cocoa powder until completely incorporated. Add sugar, brown sugar, vanilla, and salt, stirring to combine. Stir in eggs, one at a time until completely mixed through. Gently stir in flour just until incorporated and no more flour is visible. The batter will be thick.
5. Spread ⅔ of the batter evenly into the pan and set aside.

HOT FUDGE LAYER

6. In a mixing bowl, beat together the cream cheese and hot fudge until well combined. Gently spread over brownies. Spread remaining brownie batter evenly over the top.

TOPPING

7. Sprinkle with chopped peanut butter cups.
8. Bake on the center rack for 30 minutes or until brownies are set and starting to pull away slightly from the edges.
9. Allow to cool completely, and then refrigerate at least 2 hours before cutting into bars. Store refrigerated in sealed container. Makes 32 brownies.

S'MORES *Brownies*

Once you try these, you may never go back to regular s'mores again!

Ingredients

CRUST

12 full sheets graham crackers

6 Tbsp. unsalted butter (melted)

¼ cup sugar

BROWNIES

1 cup (2 sticks) unsalted butter

1¼ cups semisweet chocolate chips

¾ cup unsweetened cocoa powder

2 cups sugar

¼ cup brown sugar

1 tsp. vanilla extract

½ tsp. salt

4 eggs

1¼ cups flour

TOPPING

3½ cups mini marshmallows

GANACHE

2 Tbsp. milk (or cream)

½ cup chocolate chips

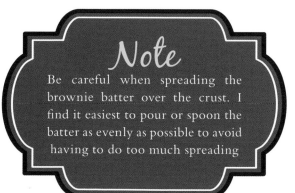

Note

Be careful when spreading the brownie batter over the crust. I find it easiest to pour or spoon the batter as evenly as possible to avoid having to do too much spreading

S'MORES  CONTINUED
Directions

1. Preheat oven to 350°F.

2. Line a 9 × 13 baking pan with foil, leaving enough to hang over the edges. Spray lightly with cooking spray.

CRUST

3. In a food processor, grind the graham crackers into fine crumbs. Add the butter and sugar, and pulse to combine. Press firmly into the bottom of the prepared pan. Bake 8 minutes.

BROWNIES

4. Meanwhile, fill a saucepan with about 2 inches of water and place a heat-safe bowl over the pan, making sure the bottom of the bowl does not touch the water. Heat the water on low until just simmering. Place butter and chocolate chips in the bowl, stirring constantly until mostly melted. Remove from heat and stir until completely melted and smooth.*

5. Stir in cocoa powder until completely incorporated. Add sugar, brown sugar, vanilla, and salt, stirring to combine. Stir in eggs, one at a time until completely mixed through. Gently stir in flour until just incorporated and no more flour is visible. The batter will be thick.

6. Very carefully spread batter evenly over the baked crust. Bake 25 minutes or until tester inserted into the center of the brownies comes out clean or with fudge crumbs.

TOPPING

7. Immediately add marshmallows to the top of the brownies and turn the oven to low broil. Bake 2–3 minutes, turning the pan every minute to ensure even toasting. Let cool completely.

8. Lift brownies from the pan and peel off foil. Cut into 28 pieces using a plastic knife to help prevent marshmallows from sticking.

GANACHE

9. For the ganache, heat the milk in a glass bowl in the microwave for 60 seconds or until barely simmering. Add chocolate and let sit for 3 minutes. Stir until melted and smooth. Spoon into a baggie and snip off a very small corner. Drizzle over brownies.

*You can also use the microwave to melt the chocolate. Place butter and chocolate chips in a glass mixing bowl and heat in the microwave in 30-second intervals, stirring between each burst, until melted and smooth.

TOFFEE *Cheesecake Brownies*

This recipe is so easy to make, but the outcome is really impressive and is always met with rave reviews!

Ingredients

BROWNIES

1 cup (2 sticks) unsalted butter

1¼ cups semisweet chocolate chips

¾ cup unsweetened cocoa powder

2 cups sugar

¼ cup brown sugar

1 tsp. vanilla extract

½ tsp. salt

4 eggs

1¼ cups flour

CHEESECAKE

8 oz. cream cheese (softened)

½ cup sugar

1 egg

1 tsp. vanilla extract

TOPPING

1 cup toffee bits
(I use Heath Baking Bits)

Directions

1. Preheat oven to 350°F.

2. Line a 9 × 13 baking pan with foil, leaving enough to hang over the edges. Spray lightly with cooking spray.

3. Fill a saucepan with about 2 inches of water. Place a heat-safe bowl over the pan, making sure the bottom of the bowl does not touch the water. Heat the water on low until just simmering. Place butter, peanut butter, and peanut butter chips in the bowl, stirring constantly until mostly melted. Remove from heat and stir until completely melted and smooth.*

4. Stir in sugar, vanilla, and salt, stirring to combine. Stir in eggs, one at a time until completely mixed through. Add baking soda, and gently stir in flour until just incorporated and no more flour is visible.

5. Spread batter evenly into the pan and top with chopped peanut butter cups. Bake on the center rack for 15 minutes or until golden and bars are starting to pull away from the edges of the pan.

6. Allow to cool completely before cutting. Store in sealed container. Makes 28 brownies.

*You can also use the microwave for melting. Place butter, peanut butter, and peanut butter chips in a glass mixing bowl and heat in the microwave in 30-second intervals, stirring between each burst, until melted and smooth.

TRIPLE CHOCOLATE BROWNIES
with Whipped Ganache

*These brownies are for the die-hard chocolate lovers (like me!).
They are sure to satisfy any chocolate craving.*

Ingredients

BROWNIES

1 cup (2 sticks) unsalted butter

1¼ cups semisweet chocolate chips

¾ cup unsweetened cocoa powder

2 cups sugar

¼ cup brown sugar

1 tsp. vanilla extract

½ tsp. salt

4 eggs

1¼ cups flour

1½ cups semisweet chocolate chips

GANACHE

⅓ cup milk (or cream)

1½ cups chocolate chips

TRIPLE CHOCOLATE BROWNIES
with Whipped Ganache CONTINUED
Directions

1. Preheat oven to 350°F.

2. Line a 9 × 13 baking pan with foil, leaving enough to hang over the edges. Spray lightly with cooking spray.

BROWNIES

3. Fill a saucepan with about 2 inches of water. Place a heat-safe bowl over the pan, making sure the bottom of the bowl does not touch the water. Heat the water on low until just simmering. Place butter and chocolate chips in the bowl, stirring constantly until mostly melted. Remove from heat and stir until completely melted and smooth.*

4. Stir in cocoa powder until completely incorporated. Add sugar, brown sugar, vanilla, and salt, stirring to combine. Stir in eggs, one at a time until completely mixed through. Gently stir in flour until just incorporated and no more flour is visible. Mix in chocolate chips. The batter will be thick.

5. Spread batter evenly into the pan and bake on the center rack for 24–28 minutes or until a tester inserted into the center of the brownies comes out clean or with fudgy crumbs.

6. Allow to cool completely before topping with ganache.

GANACHE

7. In a glass bowl, heat milk in the microwave until simmering (about 60–90 seconds). Pour in the chocolate chips, making sure the milk covers them. Let sit for 3 minutes, then stir until smooth. Let ganache cool about 20 minutes and then whip it on high until light and airy. Smooth over cooled brownies.

8. Store refrigerated in sealed container. Makes 32 brownies.

*You can also use the microwave to melt the chocolate. Place butter and chocolate chips in a glass mixing bowl and heat in the microwave in 30-second intervals, stirring between each burst, until melted and smooth.

WHITE CHOCOLATE *Fudge Brownies*

All the chewy, fudgy texture of a traditional brownie in white chocolate form!

Ingredients

BROWNIES

¾ cup (1½ sticks) unsalted butter, softened (divided)

8 oz. white chocolate chips

1⅓ cups sugar

3 eggs

1 tsp. vanilla extract

¼ tsp. almond extract

½ tsp. salt

2 cups flour

TOPPING

2 oz. white chocolate chips

sprinkles

Directions

1. Preheat oven to 350°F.

2. Line a 9 × 13 baking pan with foil, leaving enough to hang over the edges. Spray lightly with cooking spray.

BROWNIES

3. Fill a saucepan with about 2 inches of water. Place a heat-safe bowl over the pan, making sure the bottom of the bowl does not touch the water. Heat the water on low just until simmering, and place 1 stick of butter and white chocolate chips in the bowl, stirring constantly until mostly melted. Remove from heat and stir until completely melted and smooth.* Stir in remaining softened butter until mixed through.

4. Add sugar, and mix until combined. Mix in eggs, one at a time, and then stir in vanilla, almond extract, and salt. Gently stir in flour just until incorporated and no more flour is visible.

5. Spread batter evenly into the pan and bake on the center rack for 17–20 minutes or until a tester inserted into the center of the brownies comes out clean or with fudgy crumbs. Do not overbake or they will dry out and no longer be fudgy like a brownie.

6. Allow to cool completely.

TOPPING

7. In a small bowl, melt the white chocolate chip in the microwave in 20-second intervals, stirring between each burst, until melted and smooth. Place in a plastic baggie with a small corner snipped off, and quickly drizzle over brownies. Immediately add sprinkles.

8. Store in sealed container. Makes 28 brownies.

*You can also use the microwave to melt the chocolate. Place butter and chocolate chips in a glass mixing bowl and heat in the microwave in 30-second intervals, stirring between each burst, until melted and smooth.

CHAPTER TWO

Blondies

APPLE PEANUT BUTTER *Blondies* WITH CARAMEL *Peanut Butter Sauce*

Apple and peanut butter are a natural pairing, and you will fall in love with these soft, moist, flavorful blondies!

Ingredients

BLONDIES

½ cup (1 stick) unsalted butter, softened

½ cup creamy peanut butter

1½ cups brown sugar

1 egg

½ tsp. salt

2 tsp. baking powder

2¼ cups flour

1½ cups diced apples (peeled and cored)

SAUCE

⅓ cup caramel sauce

3 Tbsp. creamy peanut butter

Directions

1. Preheat oven to 350°F.

2. Line a 9 × 13 baking pan with foil, leaving enough to hang over the edges. Spray lightly with cooking spray.

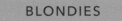

BLONDIES

3. In a mixing bowl, cream together butter, peanut butter, and sugar. Add the egg and salt, and mix well. Mix in the baking powder and flour until just combined. Stir in apples.

4. Spread into prepared pan, and bake 20–24 minutes or until tester inserted into the center of the blondies comes out clean or with crumbs. Allow to cool completely.

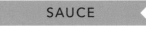

SAUCE

5. Heat the caramel and peanut butter in a glass bowl in the microwave for 20–30 seconds and stir until combined. Drizzle over blondies.

6. Makes 28 blondies. Store in a sealed container.

CARAMEL PEANUT BLONDIES
WITH *Chocolate Ganache*

These rich, decadent blondies taste like a candy bar—only better!

Ingredients

BLONDIES

½ cup (1 stick) unsalted butter, softened

1¾ cups brown sugar

½ tsp. salt

1 tsp. vanilla extract

2 eggs

2 tsp. baking powder

2 cups flour

FILLING

1 (14-oz.) bag soft caramels

2 Tbsp. water

2 cups salted peanuts

GANACHE

½ cup milk

2 cups semisweet chocolate chips

Directions

1. Preheat oven to 350°F.

2. Line a 9 × 13 baking pan with foil, leaving enough to hang over the edges. Spray lightly with cooking spray.

BLONDIES

3. In a mixing bowl, cream the butter and sugar until light and fluffy. Add the salt, vanilla, and eggs, and mix until well incorporated. Add baking powder and flour, mixing until just combined. Spread batter evenly into the prepared pan. Bake on the center rack for 24 minutes or until tester inserted in the center of the blondies comes out clean. Allow to cool completely.

FILLING

4. In a saucepan over medium low heat, melt the caramels with water, stirring frequently until smooth. Pour over blondies and immediately sprinkle with peanuts. Let cool.

GANACHE

5. Add chocolate chips to a glass bowl, set aside. Heat milk in a small saucepan on medium low until barely simmering. Pour milk over the chocolate chips, making sure the milk covers them. Let sit for 3 minutes, and then stir until smooth. Spread evenly over blondies. Let cool completely until ganache is set before cutting into blondies.

6. Store in a sealed container. Makes 32 blondies.

STEPHANIE BRUBAKER

67

MARSHMALLOW *Butterscotch Blondies*

The combination of butterscotch and peanut butter is positively addicting!
Try them warm for a gooey, chewy treat!

Ingredients

½ cup (1 stick)
unsalted butter,
softened

½ cup creamy
peanut butter

1¾ cups brown sugar

2 eggs

½ tsp. salt

1 tsp. vanilla extract

2 tsp. baking powder

2 cups flour

11 oz. butterscotch
chips

1½ cups mini
marshmallows

Directions

1. Preheat oven to 350°F.

2. Line a 9 × 13 baking pan with foil, leaving enough to hang over the edges. Spray lightly with cooking spray.

3. In a mixing bowl, cream the butter, peanut butter, and sugar until smooth. Add the eggs, one at a time, mixing between each addition. Add salt and vanilla and mix well. Add baking powder and flour, and mix until just incorporated. Stir in butterscotch and marshmallows.

4. Spread batter evenly into prepared pan. Bake on the center rack 20 minutes or until tester inserted into the center of the blondies comes out clean. Allow to cool completely before cutting into 28 blondies.

CHOCOLATE-COVERED *Potato Chip Blondies*

This may sound strange, but these blondies are a huge hit with everyone who tries them! The salty potato chip is the perfect match for the marshmallows and chocolate. These blondies have it all: salty and sweet, crunchy and chewy. Go ahead—give them a try!

Ingredients

BLONDIES

½ cup (1 stick) unsalted butter, softened

1¾ cups brown sugar

½ tsp. salt

1 tsp. vanilla extract

2 eggs

2 tsp. baking powder

2 cups flour

FILLING

4 Tbsp. unsalted butter

5 cups mini marshmallows

5 cups crushed potato chips with ridges

TOPPING

2 cups semisweet chocolate chips

Directions

1. Preheat oven to 350°F.

2. Line a 9 × 13 baking pan with foil, leaving enough to hang over the edges. Spray lightly with cooking spray.

BLONDIES

3. In a mixing bowl, cream the butter and sugar until light and fluffy. Add the salt, vanilla, and eggs, and mix until well incorporated. Add baking powder and flour, mixing until just combined.

4. Spread batter evenly into the prepared pan. Bake on the center rack for 24 minutes or until tester inserted in the center of the blondies comes out clean. Allow to cool completely.

FILLING

5. In a large pot over medium heat, melt the butter and marshmallows. Turn off heat and stir in potato chips until completely coated. Immediately drop heaping spoonfuls over the blondies, and gently press into an even layer.

TOPPING

6. Fill a saucepan with about 2 inches of water. Place a heat-safe bowl over the pan, making sure the bottom of the bowl does not touch the water. Heat the water on low until just simmering. Place chocolate chips in the bowl, stirring constantly until mostly melted. Remove from heat and stir until completely melted and smooth.*

7. Immediately pour over blondies and spread evenly.

8. Allow chocolate to set up before cutting into 32 blondies. Store in a tightly sealed container.

*You can also use the microwave to melt the chocolate. Place chocolate chips in a glass mixing bowl and heat in the microwave in 30 second intervals, stirring between each burst, until melted and smooth.

CINNAMON ROLL *Blondies*

I have a great fondness for the gooey centers of cinnamon rolls. They're the best part!
These blondies taste just like those centers but are way easier to make!

Ingredients

BLONDIES

½ cup (1 stick) unsalted butter,
softened

1¾ cups brown sugar

¾ tsp. salt

1 tsp. vanilla extract

2 eggs

2 tsp. baking powder

2 cups flour

FILLING/GLAZE

1 cup brown sugar

3 Tbsp. unsalted butter, melted

1 Tbsp. cinnamon

1 tsp. vanilla

1 Tbsp. water

FROSTING

8 oz. cream cheese, softened

6 Tbsp. unsalted butter,
softened

1 tsp. vanilla

2 cups powdered sugar

*Try warming them for
10 seconds or so in the
microwave for an ooey,
gooey treat!

Directions

1. Preheat oven to 350°F.

2. Line a 9 × 13 baking pan with foil, leaving enough to hang over the edges. Spray lightly with cooking spray.

FILLING

3. Stir together all filling ingredients and set aside.

BLONDIES

4. In a mixing bowl, cream the butter and sugar until light and fluffy. Add the salt, vanilla, and eggs, and mix until well incorporated. Add baking powder and flour, mixing until just combined. Spread batter evenly into the prepared pan. Take half of the cinnamon filling, drop spoonfuls over the blondies, and swirl with a knife. Bake on the center rack for 24 minutes or until tester inserted in the center of the blondies comes out clean. Allow to cool completely.

FROSTING

5. In a mixing bowl, beat cream cheese and butter until smooth and creamy. Add vanilla and powdered sugar, and beat until smooth and light. Spread over cooled blondies.

6. Heat the remaining cinnamon glaze in the microwave about 20 seconds or until thin enough to drizzle. Stir well, and then drizzle over blondies.

7. Keep refrigerated in a sealed container. Makes 32 blondies.

CRANBERRY *Orange Blondies*

The bright citrus of the oranges and the tartness of the cranberries perfectly complement the sweet white chocolate in these vibrant, chewy blondies!

Ingredients

½ cup (1 stick) unsalted butter, softened

1¾ cups brown sugar

2 eggs

½ tsp. salt

1 tsp. vanilla extract

zest of 2 oranges

2 Tbsp. orange juice

2 tsp. baking powder

2 cups flour

¾ cup dried cranberries

1½ cups white chocolate chips, divided

*You can also use the microwave to melt the chocolate. Place white chocolate chips in a glass mixing bowl and heat in the microwave in 30 second intervals, stirring between each burst, until melted and smooth.

Directions

1. Preheat oven to 350°F.

2. Line a 9 × 13 baking pan with foil, leaving enough to hang over the edges. Spray lightly with cooking spray.

3. In a mixing bowl, cream the butter and sugar until smooth. Add the eggs, one at a time, mixing between each addition. Add salt, vanilla, orange zest, and juice, and mix well. Add baking powder and flour, and mix until just incorporated. Stir in cranberries and 1 cup white chocolate chips.

4. Spread evenly into prepared pan, and bake on the center rack 25 minutes or until tester inserted into the center of the blondies comes out clean. Allow to cool completely before cutting.

5. Fill a saucepan about 2 inches with water. Place a heat-safe bowl over the pan, making sure the bottom of the bowl does not touch the water. Heat the water over low heat just until simmering, and place remaining white chocolate chips in the bowl, stirring constantly until mostly melted. Remove from heat and stir until completely melted and smooth.*

6. Spoon into a plastic baggie. Snip off very end of baggie, and drizzle chocolate over cooled blondies.

7. Allow chocolate to set, and then store in a sealed container. Makes 28 blondies.

FLUFFERNUTTER CHOCOLATE CHIP *Blondies*

I have made these scrumptious blondies so many times. They are so simple to make, filled with everything delicious, and are sure to become a favorite!

Ingredients

1 cup (2 sticks) unsalted butter, softened

¾ cup creamy peanut butter

1 cup brown sugar

½ cup sugar

2 eggs

½ tsp. salt

1 tsp. baking soda

2¼ cups flour

2 cups semisweet chocolate chips

1½ cups mini marshmallows

Directions

1. Preheat oven to 350°F.

2. Line a 9 × 13 baking pan with foil, leaving enough to hang over the edges. Spray lightly with cooking spray.

3. In a mixing bowl, cream together the butter, peanut butter, and sugars. Add the eggs one at a time, mixing between each addition. Add salt and baking soda, and mix again. Add flour, mixing until just incorporated. Stir in chips and marshmallows.

4. Spread into prepared pan. Bake on the center rack for 20 minutes or until golden and edges start to pull away from the sides of the pan. It will be slightly jiggly from the marshmallows but will set up as it cools. Do not overbake.

5. Allow to cool completely before cutting. Makes 28 blondies.

M&M PRETZEL *Blondies*

*I find it nearly impossible to resist the combination of salty and sweet.
These loaded blondies will keep you coming back for more!*

Ingredients

1 cup (2 sticks)
unsalted butter,
softened

1 cup brown sugar

½ cup sugar

1 egg

½ tsp. salt

2 tsp. vanilla extract

1 tsp. baking soda

2 cups flour

1 cup broken
pretzels

1 cup peanut butter
chips

1 cup M&M's

24 pretzel twists
(optional)

Directions

1. Preheat oven to 350°F.

2. Line a 9 × 13 baking pan with foil, leaving enough to hang over the edges. Spray lightly with cooking spray.

3. In a mixing bowl, cream the butter and sugars until smooth. Add the egg, salt, and vanilla, and mix well. Add baking soda and flour, and mix until just incorporated. Stir in broken pretzels, peanut butter chips, and M&M's.

4. Spread batter evenly into prepared pan. Gently press pretzel twists into the top, 4 in each row for 6 rows. Bake on the center rack 20 minutes or until tester inserted into the center of the blondies comes out clean. Allow to cool completely before cutting into 24 blondies.

5. Store in a sealed container.

PEANUT BUTTER *Cinnamon Blondies*

If you have never tried cinnamon with peanut butter, you are in for a real treat! These chewy blondies are perfectly sweet with a bit of cinnamon spice!

Ingredients

4 Tbsp. unsalted butter, softened

½ cup creamy peanut butter

1¾ cups brown sugar

2 eggs

½ tsp. salt

1 tsp. vanilla extract

½ tsp. cinnamon

2 tsp. baking powder

2 cups flour

¾ cup cinnamon chips

½ cup peanut butter chips

Directions

1. Preheat oven to 350°F.

2. Line a 9 × 13 baking pan with foil, leaving enough to hang over the edges. Spray lightly with cooking spray.

3. In a mixing bowl, cream the butter, peanut butter, and sugar until smooth. Add the eggs, one at a time, mixing between each addition. Add salt, vanilla, and cinnamon, and mix well. Add baking powder and flour, and mix until just incorporated. Stir in cinnamon and peanut butter chips.

4. Spread batter evenly into prepared pan. Bake on the center rack 16–18 minutes or until tester inserted into the center of the blondies comes out clean. Allow to cool completely before cutting into 28 blondies.

PUMPKIN PEANUT BUTTER
Cheesecake Blondies

If you haven't tried pumpkin with peanut butter yet, you are missing out!
Add chocolate chips and cheesecake to the mix and get ready to swoon!

Ingredients

BLONDIE LAYER

½ cup (1 stick) unsalted butter

¾ cup creamy peanut butter

⅔ cup pumpkin puree

1¾ cups brown sugar

1 egg

½ tsp. salt

1 tsp. vanilla extract

1 tsp. baking soda

1¾ cups flour

1 cup mini chocolate chips

CHEESECAKE LAYER

16 oz. cream cheese, softened

⅔ cup sugar

1 egg

⅓ cup pumpkin puree

½ cup mini chocolate chips

½ cup chopped walnuts

PUMPKIN PEANUT BUTTER
Cheesecake Blondies CONTINUED

Directions

1. Preheat oven to 350°F.

2. Line a 9 × 13 baking pan with foil, leaving enough to hang over the edges. Spray lightly with cooking spray

BLONDIE LAYER

3. In a mixing bowl, cream together the butter and peanut butter until smooth. Mix in the pumpkin and sugar until combined. Add egg, salt, and vanilla, and mix well. Add baking soda and flour, and mix until just combined. Stir in chocolate chips.

4. Spread into the prepared pan and set aside.

5. In a mixing bowl, cream the cream cheese and sugar until smooth. Add the egg and pumpkin, and mix until just combined. Pour evenly over cookie dough, and sprinkle with chocolate chips and walnuts.

CHEESECAKE LAYER

6. Bake on the center rack for 30–35 minutes or until only slightly jiggly. Allow to cool completely, and then cover and chill at least 2 hours.

7. Store refrigerated and covered. Makes 32 blondies.

MAPLE PECAN *Blondies*

*These blondies may appear simple, but don't be fooled—
the flavor is outstanding! Try them with a cup of coffee!*

Ingredients

BLONDIES

½ cup (1 stick) unsalted butter,
melted

1⅓ cups brown sugar

½ cup real maple syrup

3 eggs

½ tsp. salt

1 tsp. vanilla extract

½ tsp. maple extract

2 tsp. baking powder

2 cups flour

1 cup chopped pecans

GLAZE

1 cup powdered sugar

3 Tbsp. real maple syrup

pinch of salt

2 Tbsp. water

28 whole pecans

MAPLE PECAN *Blondies* CONTINUED

Directions

1. Preheat oven to 350°F.

2. Line a 9 × 13 baking pan with foil, leaving enough to hang over the edges. Spray lightly with cooking spray.

BLONDIES

3. In a mixing bowl, cream the butter, sugar, and maple syrup until smooth. Add the eggs, one at a time, mixing between each addition. Add salt, vanilla, and maple extract, and mix well. Add baking powder and flour, and mix until just incorporated. Stir in pecans.

4. Spread evenly into prepared pan and bake on the center rack 24 minutes or until tester inserted into the center of the blondies comes out clean. Allow to cool completely before cutting into 28 blondies.

GLAZE

5. Combine sugar, syrup, maple extract, salt, and 1 tablespoon water into a bowl. Stir until combined and smooth. If too thick, add more water 1 teaspoon at a time until desired consistency is reached (should be the texture of glue). Spoon a bit of glaze on top of each bar and top immediately with a pecan. Allow glaze to set up before storing in a sealed container.

*You can also use the microwave to melt the chocolate. Place chocolate chips in a glass mixing bowl and heat in the microwave in 30 second intervals, stirring between each burst, until melted and smooth.

SNICKERDOODLE *Blondies*

Who doesn't love a good snickerdoodle? These soft and chewy blondies have become a family favorite—and they're so much faster to make than snickerdoodle cookies!

Ingredients

BLONDIES

1 cup (2 sticks) unsalted butter, softened

2 cups brown sugar

2 eggs

½ tsp. salt

2 tsp. vanilla extract

2 tsp. baking powder

2⅔ cups flour

TOPPING

2 Tbsp. sugar

2 tsp. cinnamon

Directions

1. Preheat oven to 350°F.

2. Line a 9 × 13 baking pan with foil, leaving enough to hang over the edges. Spray lightly with cooking spray.

3. In a mixing bowl, cream together the butter and sugar. Add the eggs one at a time, mixing between each addition. Add salt and vanilla, and mix again. Add baking powder and flour, mixing until just incorporated. Spread batter into prepared pan and set aside.

4. In a small bowl, stir together the cinnamon and sugar. Sprinkle evenly over blondies. Bake on center rack for 20 minutes or until tester comes out with moist crumbs. Do not overbake.

5. Allow to cool before cutting into 28 blondies.

MAGIC *Blondie Bars*

These over-the-top, gooey, chewy blondies are the ultimate treat for your sweet tooth!

Ingredients

BLONDIES

½ cup (1 stick) unsalted butter, softened

1½ cups brown sugar

½ tsp. salt

2 tsp. vanilla extract

2 eggs

2 tsp. baking powder

2 cups flour

TOPPING

½ cup mini Reese's Pieces

1½ cups M&M's, divided

1 cup milk chocolate chips

1 cup peanut butter chips

1 (14 oz.) can sweetened condensed milk

Directions

1. Preheat oven to 350°F.

2. Line a 9 × 13 baking pan with foil, leaving enough to hang over the edges. Spray lightly with cooking spray.

BLONDIES

3. In a mixing bowl, cream the butter and sugar until light and fluffy. Add the salt, vanilla, and eggs, and mix until well incorporated. Add baking powder and flour, mixing until just combined. Spread batter evenly into the prepared pan and bake 15 minutes.

TOPPING

4. Immediately top blondies with Reese's, ¾ cup M&M's, and milk chocolate and peanut butter chips. Pour condensed milk on top, as evenly as possible. Bake 15–20 more minutes. Immediately sprinkle with remaining ¾ cup M&M's. Cool completely before cutting into 32 blondies.

5. Store in a sealed container.

CHAPTER THREE

Bars

BROWN BUTTER *Oatmeal Raisin Bars*

Brown butter makes everything better! It gives these bars a chewy texture and rich nutty flavor. The cream cheese frosting puts these over the edge!

Ingredients

BARS

1 cup (2 sticks) unsalted butter, browned and slightly cooled*

1 cup brown sugar

2 tsp. vanilla extract

2 eggs

½ tsp. salt

1 tsp. cinnamon

¼ tsp. cloves

½ tsp. nutmeg

1 tsp. baking soda

1½ cups flour

2 cups old fashioned oats

1½ cups raisins

FROSTING

8 oz. cream cheese, softened

6 Tbsp. unsalted butter, softened

1 tsp. vanilla

2 cups powdered sugar

*To brown butter, place in a saucepan over medium heat, stirring as it melts. Once melted, stop stirring and watch closely for the butter to turn a rich, golden brown (about 7–10 minutes). It will bubble and foam and smell nutty, and dark bits will develop. As soon as it turns brown, remove from heat—at this point it will burn quickly if you're not careful!

BROWN BUTTER *Oatmeal Raisin Bars* CONTINUED

Directions

1. Preheat oven to 350°F.

2. Line a 9 × 13 baking pan with foil, leaving enough to hang over the edges. Spray lightly with cooking spray.

BARS

3. In a mixing bowl, beat the butter and sugar. Add the vanilla, eggs, salt, cinnamon, cloves, and nutmeg until well combined. Add baking soda and flour, mixing until just combined. Stir in oats and raisins.

4. Spread batter evenly into the prepared pan. Bake on the center rack for 15 minutes or until tester inserted in the center of the bars comes out clean. Allow to cool completely.

FROSTING

5. In a mixing bowl, beat cream cheese and butter until smooth and creamy. Add vanilla and powdered sugar, and beat until smooth and light. Spread or pipe over cooled bars.

6. Keep refrigerated in a sealed container. Makes 28 bars.

BROWNIE STUFFED *Krispie Treats* WITH SALTED *Caramel*

These over-the-top treats are impossible to resist! With all the different flavors and textures, it's like a party in your mouth!

Ingredients

BROWNIES

½ cup (1 stick) unsalted butter

½ cup semisweet chocolate chips

⅓ cup unsweetened cocoa powder

1 cup sugar

2 Tbsp. brown sugar

½ tsp. vanilla extract

¼ tsp. salt

2 eggs

¾ cup flour

KRISPIE TREATS

8 cups mini marshmallows

4 Tbsp. unsalted butter

8 cups puffed rice cereal

TOPPING

¼ cup caramel sauce

½ tsp. coarse ground sea salt

BROWNIE STUFFED *Krispie Treats* WITH SALTED *Caramel* CONTINUED
Directions

1. Preheat oven to 350°F.

2. Line a 8 × 8 baking pan with foil, leaving enough to hang over the edges. Spray lightly with cooking spray.

BROWNIES

3. Fill a saucepan with about 2 inches of water. Place a heat-safe bowl over the pan, making sure the bottom of the bowl does not touch the water. Heat the water on low until just simmering. Place butter and chocolate chips in the bowl, stirring constantly until mostly melted. Remove from heat and stir until completely melted and smooth.*

4. Stir in cocoa powder until completely incorporated. Add sugar, brown sugar, vanilla, and salt, stirring to combine. Stir in eggs, one at a time until completely mixed through. Gently stir in flour until just incorporated and no more flour is visible. The batter will be thick.

5. Spread batter evenly into the pan and bake on the center rack for 24–28 minutes or until a tester inserted into the center of the brownies comes out clean or with fudgy crumbs.

6. Allow to cool completely and then cut into bite-sized pieces. Freeze in a single layer on a baking sheet for at least 1 hour.

KRISPIE TREATS

7. In a large pot over medium heat, melt the marshmallows and butter, stirring constantly. Once melted, turn off heat and stir in cereal until well coated.

8. Gently press half of the mixture into a greased 9 × 13 pan. Sprinkle evenly with frozen brownies and quickly and firmly press remaining cereal mixture on top using damp fingers.

TOPPING

9. Heat the caramel sauce until pourable and stir in sea salt. Drizzle over bars. Allow bars to set up before cutting into 32 bars.

10. Store in a tightly sealed container.

*You can also use the microwave to melt the chocolate. Place butter and chocolate chips in a glass mixing bowl and heat in the microwave in 30-second intervals, stirring between each burst, until melted and smooth.

CANNOLI CREAM *Cookie Bars*

*Creamy, dreamy cannoli cream has made a new best friend
in these chewy chocolate chip cookie bars!*

Ingredients

CANNOLI CREAM

12 oz. strained Ricotta cheese

8 oz. Mascarpone cheese

1 cup powdered sugar

½ tsp. almond extract

⅓ cup mini semisweet chocolate
chips (for garnish)

COOKIE LAYER

¾ cup (1½ sticks) unsalted butter,
softened

¾ cup brown sugar

½ cup sugar

1 egg

1 tsp. vanilla extract

½ tsp. salt

1 Tbsp. cornstarch

1 tsp. baking soda

1¾ cups flour

1½ cups semisweet chocolate
chips

CHOCOLATE *Carmelitas* CONTINUED

Directions

1. Line a 9 × 13 baking pan with foil, leaving enough to hang over the edges. Spray lightly with cooking spray.

COOKIE LAYER

2. In a mixing bowl, cream together butter and sugar. Add cocoa powder and mix well. Mix in eggs one at a time. Add salt and baking soda, and mix again. With the mixer on low, gradually add in the oats and flour until just combined. Press half of the dough into prepared pan, and set aside.

FILLING

3. In a small saucepan over medium heat, melt the caramels with milk, stirring frequently. As soon as it is melted and smooth, remove from heat and pour over dough, reserving $\frac{1}{3}$ cup for topping. Sprinkle chocolate chips over the caramel.

4. Take spoonfuls of remaining dough and flatten with your hands (put cooking spray on your hands or use 2 pieces of wax paper). Lay dough as evenly as possible over the caramel. Bake 25 minutes.

5. Allow to cool completely before cutting. Heat remaining caramel until thin enough to pour, and drizzle over bars.

6. Store in a sealed container. Makes 32 bars.

CHOCOLATE CHEESECAKE *Cookie Bars*

*Rich and creamy chocolate cheesecake surrounded by
layers of chocolate chip cookie bars–heavenly!*

Ingredients

COOKIE LAYER

1 cup (2 sticks) unsalted butter,
softened

1 cup brown sugar

⅓ cup sugar

1 tsp. vanilla extract

½ tsp. salt

2 eggs

1 tsp. baking soda

2 cups flour

1 (12-oz.) bag semisweet
chocolate chips

CHEESECAKE LAYER

16 oz. cream cheese, softened

⅓ cup sugar

1 cup semisweet chocolate chips,
melted and slightly cooled*

2 eggs

*You can also use the microwave to melt the
chocolate. Place chocolate chips in a glass mixing
bowl and heat in the microwave in 30-second
intervals, stirring between each burst, until
melted and smooth.

CHOCOLATE CHEESECAKE
Cookie Bars CONTINUED

Directions

1. Preheat oven to 350°F.

2. Line a 9 × 13 baking pan with foil, leaving enough to hang over the edges. Spray lightly with cooking spray.

COOKIE LAYER

3. In a mixing bowl, cream together the butter and sugars. Add vanilla, salt, and eggs, and mix well. Mix in the baking soda and flour until just combined. Stir in chips. Press ⅔ dough into the prepared pan and set aside.

CHEESECAKE LAYER

4. In a mixing bowl, beat the softened cream cheese and sugar until light and creamy. Add the melted chocolate, and mix until combined. Mix in eggs on low just until incorporated. Do not over mix.

5. Spread cheesecake layer evenly over cookie dough. Take spoonfuls of remaining cookie dough and flatten with your hands (put cooking spray on your hands or use 2 pieces of wax paper). Lay as evenly as possible over the cheesecake layer. Bake 30–35 minutes on center rack or until bars are golden and mostly set.

6. Allow to cool completely, and then refrigerate at least 3 hours. Store refrigerated in sealed container. Makes 32 bars.

CINNAMON *Swirl Bars*

*These soft and fluffy bars taste a lot like cinnamon rolls,
but they are so much faster and easier to make!*

Ingredients

BARS

8 oz. cream cheese, softened
¾ cup (1½ sticks) unsalted butter
¾ cup sugar
½ cup brown sugar
1 egg
½ tsp. salt
1 tsp. vanilla
1 tsp. almond extract
1 tsp. baking soda
½ Tbsp. cornstarch
2 cups flour

TOPPING

6 Tbsp. unsalted butter, softened
½ cup brown sugar
½ Tbsp. cinnamon
2 Tbsp. flour

GLAZE

1 cup powdered sugar
2 tsp. milk

CINNAMON *Swirl Bars* CONTINUED

Directions

1. Preheat oven to 350°F.

2. Line a 9 × 13 baking pan with foil, leaving enough to hang over the edges. Spray lightly with cooking spray.

BARS

3. In a mixing bowl, cream together the cream cheese, butter, and sugars. Add the egg, salt, vanilla, and almond extract, and mix well. Add baking soda, cornstarch, and flour, and mix until just combined. Spread into prepared pan and set aside.

TOPPING

4. In a mixing bowl, beat together the butter, sugar, cinnamon, and flour. Drop by spoonfuls over bars and swirl with a knife. Bake on center rack for 18 minutes or until tester inserted into the center of the bars comes out clean. Let cool slightly.

GLAZE

5. In a bowl, stir together the sugar and milk until smooth. If the glaze is too thick, add more milk 1 teaspoon at a time until desired consistency is reached. Drizzle over bars.

6. Makes 28 bars. Store in a sealed container.

NO BAKE OREO PEANUT BUTTER *Cheesecake Bars*

When you make these luscious bars, be prepared for rave reviews and many recipe requests. They are absolutely heavenly!

Ingredients

CRUST

½ cup (1 stick) unsalted butter, melted

2½ cups (25 Oreos) Oreo cookie crumbs

16 oz. warmed hot fudge, divided

FILLING

8 oz. cream cheese, softened

¾ cup creamy peanut butter

1½ cups powdered sugar

8 oz. Cool Whip

Directions

1. Line a 9 × 13 baking pan with foil, leaving enough to hang over the edges. Spray lightly with cooking spray.

CRUST

2. In a large bowl stir together the butter and cookie crumbs. Press firmly into prepared pan and chill 10 minutes. Spread with warmed hot fudge (minus ¼ cup) and chill.

FILLING

3. In a mixing bowl beat cream cheese with peanut butter until smooth and creamy. Mix in powdered sugar. Fold in Cool Whip until well incorporated. Spread over chilled crust.

4. Heat remaining hot fudge and drizzle over bars. Chill at least 4 hours before cutting.

5. Makes 28 bars. Store refrigerated in a sealed container.

CHOCOLATE *Pecan Pie Bars*

This is probably my husband's favorite recipe in this book! We love these so much that they have become a new Thanksgiving tradition!

Ingredients

CRUST

1 cup (2 sticks) unsalted butter, cold and cubed

⅓ cup powdered sugar

1¼ cups flour

FILLING

14 oz. sweetened condensed milk

3 Tbsp. unsweetened cocoa powder

2 cups semisweet chocolate chips

1 (8-oz.) bag pecan halves

TOPPING

⅓ cup mini chocolate chips

Directions

1. Preheat oven to 350°F.

2. Line a 9 × 13 baking pan with foil, leaving enough to hang over the edges. Spray lightly with cooking spray.

CRUST

3. In a large bowl, using a pastry cutter or fork, cut butter into sugar and flour until crumbly. Press evenly into prepared pan and bake on the center rack 12 minutes.

FILLING

4. In a mixing bowl, stir together condensed milk and cocoa until well combined. Set aside.

5. Sprinkle chocolate chips and pecans over the cooked crust, and pour chocolate condensed milk evenly over the top. Bake 15–18 minutes. Immediately sprinkle with mini chocolate chips.

TOPPING

6. Allow to cool completely before cutting into 28 bars. Store in a tightly sealed container.

LEMON BLUEBERRY *Cream Bars*

When I'm not craving chocolate, I've got lemon on my mind! Lemon and blueberry are a match made in heaven, and this luscious dessert is divine!

Ingredients

LEMON CURD

¾ cup sugar

4 Tbsp. unsalted butter, softened

2 eggs

¼ cup fresh lemon juice

CRUST

½ cup (1 stick) unsalted butter, softened

1¼ cups sugar

1 tsp. vanilla extract

¼ tsp. salt

1 egg

zest of 1 lemon

1 Tbsp. fresh lemon juice

½ tsp. baking powder

1½ cups flour

CREAM

8 oz. cream cheese, softened

1½ cups powdered sugar

1 tsp. vanilla extract

8 oz. Cool Whip

1 cup blueberries

zest of 1 lemon

Directions

1. Preheat oven to 350°F.

2. Line a 9 × 13 baking pan with foil, leaving enough to hang over the edges. Spray lightly with cooking spray. Set aside.

LEMON CURD

3. In a mixing bowl, cream together the sugar and butter. Add eggs and lemon juice, and mix well. Pour into a saucepan and cook over low heat, stirring often, until thick and barely simmering (about 10 minutes). Let cool slightly. Pour into a container and chill at least an hour.

CRUST

4. In a mixing bowl, cream the butter and sugar until light and fluffy. Add the vanilla, salt, egg, zest, and lemon juice, and mix until well incorporated. Add the baking powder and flour, mixing until just combined.

5. Press dough evenly into the pan and bake on the center rack for 12 minutes. Allow to cool completely, and then spread cooled lemon curd over crust.

CREAM

6. In a mixing bowl, beat the cream cheese, sugar, and vanilla until smooth and creamy. Fold in Cool Whip and spread over bars. Sprinkle with blueberries and lemon zest. Cover and chill 2 hours.

7. Store refrigerated in a sealed container. Makes 28 bars.

NEAPOLITAN COOKIE *Bars*

Two layers of chewy cookies topped with a smooth white chocolate ganache inspired by Neapolitan ice cream!

Ingredients

CHOCOLATE LAYER

½ cup (1 stick) unsalted butter, softened

1¼ cups sugar

½ cup unsweetened cocoa powder

¼ tsp. salt

1 tsp. vanilla extract

1 egg

½ tsp. baking powder

1¼ cups flour

¾ cup mini chocolate chips

STRAWBERRY LAYER

⅔ cup chopped strawberries

1 ¼ cups sugar

½ cup (1 stick) unsalted butter, softened

¼ tsp. salt

½ tsp. strawberry extract

1 egg

½ tsp. baking powder

1 ¾ cups flour

4 drops red food color (optional)

GANACHE

⅓ cup milk

2 cups white chocolate chips

NEAPOLITAN *Cookie Bars* CONTINUED

Directions

1. Preheat oven to 350°F.

2. Line a 9 × 13 baking pan with foil, leaving enough to hang over the edges. Spray lightly with cooking spray.

CHOCOLATE LAYER

3. In a mixing bowl, cream the butter and sugar until light and fluffy. Add the cocoa powder and mix well. Add the salt, vanilla, and egg and mix until well incorporated. Add baking powder and flour, mixing until just combined. Stir in chocolate chips.

4. Press into prepared pan and set aside.

STRAWBERRY LAYER

5. In a glass bowl, mash the strawberries with the sugar. In a mixing bowl, cream the butter until light and fluffy. Mix in the strawberry-sugar mixture until well combined. Add the salt, strawberry extract, and egg, and mix until well incorporated. Add baking powder and flour mixing until just combined. Stir in food coloring. Carefully spread over chocolate layer and bake on the center rack for 25–28 minutes or until tester inserted in the center of the bars comes out clean. Allow to cool completely.

GANACHE

6. In a microwave, heat milk in a glass bowl for 60–90 seconds or until just simmering. Pour in chocolate chips, making sure they are covered with the milk, and let sit for 3 minutes. Stir until melted and smooth. Let cool slightly, and then pour over cooled bars. Allow ganache to set before cutting into bars.

7. Store in a sealed container. Makes 32 bars.

EGGNOG MELTAWAY *Bars*

These light, dreamy bars literally melt in your mouth!
A beautiful treat for the Christmas tray!

Ingredients

BARS

¾ cup (1½ sticks) unsalted butter, softened

½ cup eggnog

1 cup sugar

½ tsp. salt

1 egg

¼ tsp. baking soda

¼ tsp. baking powder

2 cups flour

GLAZE

2 cups powdered sugar

pinch of salt

5 Tbsp. eggnog*

*Whole milk can be substituted for the eggnog so this treat can be enjoyed year round!

Directions

1. Preheat oven to 350°F.

2. Line a 9 × 13 baking pan with foil, leaving enough to hang over the edges. Spray lightly with cooking spray.

BARS

3. In a mixing bowl, cream together the butter, eggnog, and sugar. Add the salt and egg, and mix until well incorporated. Add the baking soda, baking powder, and 1 cup flour, mixing until just combined. Mix in remaining flour.

4. Spread batter evenly into the pan and bake on the center rack for 15–17 minutes or until tester inserted in the center of the bars comes out clean. Allow to cool completely.

GLAZE

5. In a mixing bowl, stir together sugar, salt, and eggnog until smooth and looks like the texture of glue.

6. Cut bars into 28 squares, and set them on wax paper with a bit of space between each bar. Pour glaze over bars. Allow glaze to set up before storing in a sealed container.

FUNFETTI CREAM CHEESE *Bars*

These fun bars are soft, light, and bursting with color!
Change up the color of sprinkles to match any occasion.

Ingredients

8 oz. cream cheese, softened

10 Tbsp. unsalted butter, softened

½ cup brown sugar

½ cup sugar

½ tsp. salt

1 egg

2 tsp. vanilla extract

½ Tbsp. cornstarch

1 tsp. baking soda

2 cups flour

⅓ cup + 2 Tbsp. rainbow sprinkles

Directions

1. Preheat oven to 350°F.

2. Line a 9 × 13 baking pan with foil, leaving enough to hang over the edges. Spray lightly with cooking spray.

3. In a mixing bowl, cream the cream cheese, butter, and the sugars until light and fluffy. Add the salt, egg, and vanilla, and mix until well incorporated. Add cornstarch and baking soda, and mix again. Add the flour, mixing until just combined. Stir in ⅓ cup sprinkles until evenly distributed.

4. Spread batter evenly into the pan, and add remaining sprinkles on top. Bake on the center rack for 18 minutes or until tester inserted in the center of the bars comes out clean. Allow to cool completely.

5. Store in a sealed container. Makes 28 bars.

NO BAKE PEANUT BUTTER CUP
Bars with Oreo Crust

I will warn you right now: these bars are dangerous. They are seriously addicting, since they are so easy to make and require no baking!

Ingredients

CRUST

½ cup (1 stick) unsalted butter, melted

2½ cups Oreo cookie crumbs

FILLING

½ cup (1 stick) unsalted butter, softened

1½ cups creamy peanut butter

3 cups powdered sugar

1 tsp. vanilla extract

¼ tsp. salt

TOPPING

2 cups milk chocolate chips

Directions

1. Line a 9 × 13 baking pan with foil, leaving enough to hang over the edges. Spray lightly with cooking spray.

CRUST

2. In a large bowl stir together the melted butter and cookie crumbs until well combined. Press firmly into prepared pan and chill 10 minutes.

FILLING

3. In a mixing bowl beat the butter and peanut butter until creamy. Add sugar, vanilla, and salt, and mix well. Press evenly on top of chilled cookie crust.

TOPPING

4. Fill a saucepan about 2 inches with water. Place a heat-safe bowl over the pan, making sure the bottom of the bowl does not touch the water. Heat the water over low heat just until simmering, and place chocolate chips in the bowl, stirring constantly until mostly melted.* Remove from heat and stir until completely melted and smooth. Immediately spread over filling. Allow to cool and set up before cutting. Makes 32 bars.

*You can also use the microwave to melt the chocolate. Place butter and chocolate chips in a glass mixing bowl and heat in the microwave in 30-second intervals, stirring between each burst, until melted and smooth.

PEANUT BUTTER *Fudge Bars*

Chocolate and peanut butter is a combination I just can't resist.
This is one of my all-time favorite recipes, and I think it will be one of yours too!

Ingredients

COOKIE LAYER

1 cup (2 sticks) unsalted butter, softened

⅓ cup creamy peanut butter

1 cup brown sugar

½ cup sugar

1 tsp. vanilla extract

½ tsp. salt

1 egg

1 tsp. baking soda

2 cups flour

1 (10-oz.) bag peanut butter chips

FUDGE LAYER

1 (14-oz.) can sweetened condensed milk

1 (12-oz.) bag semisweet chocolate chips

PEANUT BUTTER *Fudge Bars* CONTINUED

Directions

1. Preheat oven to 350°F.

2. Line a 9 × 13 baking pan with foil, leaving enough to hang over the edges. Spray lightly with cooking spray.

COOKIE LAYER

3. In a mixing bowl, cream the butter, peanut butter, and sugars until light and fluffy. Add the vanilla, salt, and egg, and mix well. Mix in the baking soda and flour until just combined. Stir in peanut butter chips.

4. Press ⅔ dough into prepared pan. Set aside.

FUDGE LAYER

5. In a glass bowl, heat the condensed milk and chocolate chips in the microwave in 30-second intervals, stirring between each burst until melted and smooth. Immediately spread over cookie dough.

6. Take spoonfuls of remaining cookie dough and flatten with your hands (put cooking spray on your hands or use 2 pieces of wax paper). Lay as evenly as possible over the fudge.

7. Bake for 22–25 minutes or until golden and edges start to slightly pull away from the sides.

8. Allow to cool completely. Refrigerate until set (about 2 hours). Store in sealed container. Makes 32 bars.

PEPPERMINT MOCHA *Bars*

These bars were inspired by my favorite coffee house drink. They are thick and chewy with cool and creamy peppermint frosting. Amazing!

Ingredients

BARS

1 cup (2 sticks) unsalted butter, softened

½ cup brown sugar

1 cup sugar

½ cup unsweetened cocoa powder

2 eggs

1 tsp. peppermint extract

½ tsp. salt

2 Tbsp. strong brewed coffee

2 Tbsp. cornstarch

1 tsp. baking soda

2 cups flour

12 oz. semisweet chocolate chips

FROSTING

½ cup (1 stick) unsalted butter, softened

2½ cups powdered sugar

1 tsp. peppermint extract

3–4 Tbsp. cream

4 drops red food coloring (optional)

2 Tbsp. candy canes, crushed (optional)

PEPPERMINT MOCHA *Bars* CONTINUED

Directions

1. Preheat oven to 350°F.

2. Line a 9 × 13 baking pan with foil leaving enough to hang over the edges. Spray lightly with cooking spray.

BARS

3. In a mixing bowl, cream the butter and the sugars until light and fluffy. Add the cocoa powder, and mix well. Add the eggs, peppermint, salt, and coffee, and mix until well incorporated. Add cornstarch and baking soda, and mix again. Add the flour, mixing until just combined. Stir in chocolate chips.

4. Press dough evenly into the pan and bake on the center rack for 22–24 minutes or until tester inserted in the center of the bars comes out clean. Allow to cool completely.

FROSTING

5. In a mixing bowl, beat butter, sugar, peppermint and 3 tablespoons of cream until smooth and fluffy. If too thick, add more cream 1 teaspoon at a time until desired consistency is reached. Stir in 4 drops of red food coloring, if desired. Spread or pipe over cooled bars, and immediately sprinkle with candy canes.

6. Keep refrigerated in a sealed container. Makes 32 bars.

RED VELVET Chocolate Chip Bars

*These thick, chewy bars are loaded with chocolate chips,
and the color really makes a statement!*

Ingredients

1 cup (2 sticks) unsalted
butter, softened

1½ cups sugar

2 eggs

3 Tbsp. unsweetened
cocoa powder

½ tsp. salt

1 tsp. vanilla extract

1 tsp. white vinegar

1 tsp. baking powder

2 cups flour

1½ Tbsp. red food
coloring

2 cups semisweet
chocolate chips

Directions

1. Preheat oven to 350°F.

2. Line a 9 × 13 baking pan with foil, leaving enough to hang over the edges. Spray lightly with cooking spray.

3. In a mixing bowl, cream the butter and sugar until light and fluffy. Add the eggs, one at a time, mixing well between each addition. Add the cocoa, salt, vanilla, and vinegar, and mix until well combined. Mix in the baking powder and flour until just incorporated. Add food coloring and mix until evenly distributed. Stir in chocolate chips.

4. Spread evenly into prepared pan and bake on the center rack 22–24 minutes or until tester inserted into the center of the bars comes out clean.

5. Allow to cool completely. Store in sealed container. Makes 28 bars.

S'MORES *Bars*

All the goodness of a s'more in an outrageous cookie bar.
You will definitely want s'more of these!

Ingredients

CRUST

10 graham cracker sheets

½ cup (1 stick) unsalted butter, melted

BARS

¾ cup (1½ sticks) unsalted butter, softened

1½ cups brown sugar

1 egg

½ tsp. salt

1 tsp. vanilla extract

1 tsp. baking soda

2 cups flour

2 cups semisweet chocolate chips

1 cup (3 sheets) graham crackers broken into bite-sized pieces

1½ cups mini marshmallows

Directions

1. Preheat oven to 350°F.

2. Line a 9 × 13 baking pan with foil, leaving enough to hang over the edges. Spray lightly with cooking spray.

CRUST

3. In a food processor, pulse graham crackers into fine crumbs. Add melted butter and pulse until evenly distributed. Firmly press crumbs into prepared pan, and bake on center rack for 10 minutes.

BARS

4. In a mixing bowl, cream the butter and sugar until light and fluffy. Add the egg, salt, and vanilla, and mix well. Add baking soda and flour, and mix until just incorporated. Stir in chocolate chips, graham crackers, and marshmallows.

5. Spread evenly into prepared pan and bake on the center rack 23–25 minutes or until golden and edges start to pull away from the pan.

6. Allow to cool completely before cutting into 28 bars. Store in sealed container.

TOASTED COCONUT LIME *Cheesecake Bars*

These creamy bars will transport you to a tropical island. The luscious lime cheesecake sits on a buttery, toasted coconut, shortbread crust that is just amazing!

Ingredients

CRUST

¾ cup (1½ sticks) unsalted butter, cold

⅓ cup powdered sugar

1¼ cups flour

1⅓ cups toasted coconut, divided*

CHEESECAKE

10 oz. cream cheese, softened

1½ cups sugar

2 eggs

½ cup lime juice

¼ cup flour

1½ tsp. baking powder

*To toast coconut, preheat oven 350°F. Place shredded coconut on a baking sheet and bake for 5 minutes, stirring every 2 minutes to ensure even toasting.

TOASTED COCONUT LIME
Cheesecake Bars CONTINUED

Directions

1. Preheat oven to 350°F.

2. Line a 9 × 13 baking pan with foil, leaving enough to hang over the edges. Spray lightly with cooking spray.

CRUST

3. In a mixing bowl, cut the butter, sugar, and flour together until beads of buttery dough form. Add 1 cup toasted coconut and stir. Press dough evenly into the pan and bake on the center rack for 10 minutes.

CHEESECAKE

4. In a mixing bowl, beat the cream cheese and sugar until smooth and creamy. Add the eggs, one at a time, mixing between each addition. Stir in lime juice. Add flour and baking powder, and mix until just combined. Pour evenly over baked crust and bake on center rack for 28–30 minutes or until mostly set (cheesecake still jiggles slightly in the center). Allow to cool completely. Cover and refrigerate at least 2–4 hours before serving.

5. Garnish with whipped cream and remaining toasted coconut, if desired.

6. Store refrigerated in a sealed container. Makes 32 bars.

WHITE CHOCOLATE DIPPED *Molasses Bars*

These warm, spicy bars balance perfectly with the sweet white chocolate, making them a holiday favorite in my family!

Ingredients

BARS

1 cup (2 sticks) unsalted butter, softened

1 cup brown sugar

2 eggs

½ cup molasses

½ tsp. salt

1 tsp. vanilla extract

2 tsp. ginger

1 tsp. cinnamon

½ tsp. nutmeg

1 tsp. baking soda

2¾ cups flour

2 Tbsp. sugar

TOPPING

8 oz. white melting chocolate

sprinkles or sugar crystals

WHITE CHOCOLATE DIPPED
Molasses Bars CONTINUED

Directions

1. Preheat oven to 350°F.

2. Line a 9 × 13 baking pan with foil, leaving enough to hang over the edges. Spray lightly with cooking spray.

BARS

3. In a mixing bowl, cream the butter and sugar until light and fluffy. Add the eggs, molasses, salt, vanilla, ginger, cinnamon, and nutmeg, and mix well. Add baking soda and flour, and mix until just incorporated.

4. Spread evenly into prepared pan and sprinkle with sugar. Bake on the center rack 15–17 minutes or until tester inserted into the center of the bars comes out clean. Do not overbake or they will not be soft and chewy.

5. Allow to cool completely before cutting. Makes 24 bars.

TOPPING

6. Fill a saucepan with about 2 inches of water. Place a heat-safe bowl over the pan, making sure the bottom of the bowl does not touch the water. Heat the water on low until just simmering. Place white chocolate in the bowl, stirring constantly until mostly melted. Remove from heat and stir until completely melted and smooth.* Carefully dip ends of bars into the chocolate and immediately add sprinkles. Lay dipped bars on wax paper and let chocolate harden before storing in a sealed container.

*You can also use the microwave to melt the white chocolate. Place white chocolate chips in a glass mixing bowl and heat in the microwave in 30-second intervals, stirring between each burst, until melted and smooth.

Index

A

Apple Peanut Butter Blondies 64

B

Back for Seconds Brownies 8
Banana Split Brownies 17
Brown Butter Oatmeal Raisin Bars 97
Brownie Stuffed Krispie Treats 99

C

Cannoli Cream Cookie Bars 103
Caramel Peanut Blondies 67
Caramel Peanut Butter Sauce 64
        See also Apple Peanut Butter Blondies
Cherry Cordial Brownies 14
Chocolate Carmelitas 105
Chocolate Cheesecake Cookie Bars 108
Chocolate Chip Cookie
        Stuffed Brownies 20
Chocolate-Covered Potato
        Chip Blondies 70
Chocolate Ganache 67
        See also Caramel Peanut Blondies
Chocolate Pecan Pie Bars 116
Cinnamon Roll Blondies 73
Cinnamon Swirl Bars 111
Coconut Almond Fudge Brownies 11

Coconut Macaroon Brownies 23
Coffee Toffee Brownies 26
Cranberry Orange Blondies 76

D

Dark Chocolate Raspberry Brownies 29

E

Eggnog Meltaway Bars 125

F

Fluffernutter Chocolate Chip Blondies 79
Funfetti Cream Cheese Bars 126

G

Glazed Lemon Brownies 32

H

Hot Fudge Peanut Butter Cup Cheesecake
        Brownies 44

L

Lemon Blueberry Cream Bars 119

M

Magic Blondie Bars 93
Maple Pecan Blondies 87
Marshmallow Butterscotch Blondies 68
Mint Fudge Stuffed Brownies 35
M&M Pretzel Blondies 81

N

Neapolitan Cookie Bars 121
No Bake Oreo Peanut
      Butter Cheesecake Bars 114
No Bake Peanut Butter Cup
 Bars with Oreo Crust 129
Nutella Brownies with a Pretzel Crust 38
Nutella Frosting 26
      See also Coffee Toffee Brownies

O

Oreo Mousse Brownies 41

P

Peanut Butter Cinnamon Blondies 83
Peanut Butter Fudge Bars 130
Peanut Butter Supreme Brownies 53

Peppermint Mocha Bars 133
Pumpkin Peanut Butter Cheesecake
      Blondies 84

R

Red Velvet Chocolate Chip Bars 136

S

Salted Caramel 99
      See also Brownie Stuffed Krispie Treats
S'mores Bars 138
S'mores Brownies 47
Snickerdoodle Blondies 91

T

Toasted Coconut Lime Cheesecake Bars 140
Toffee Cheesecake Brownies 50
Triple Chocolate Brownies 56

W

Whipped Ganache 56
      See also Triple Chocolate Brownies
White Chocolate Dipped Molasses Bars 143
White Chocolate Fudge Brownies 59

ABOUT THE *Author*

STEPHANIE BRUBAKER lives in the Midwest with her husband and four (soon to be five) young children. She is passionate about baking and has developed recipes for several national brands. She is the author of the popular blog *Back for Seconds* and is a regular contributor to *Parade's Community Table*. Her recipes and photographs have been featured in publications such as *Ladies Home Journal, Shape, Better Homes and Gardens,* and many more.